Title: "Echoes of '82: The Story of the S[

Introduction

Football is more than a sport. It is a language of passion spoken in every corner of the globe, a ritual that binds generations, and a stage where nations rise and legends are born. Every four years, the world pauses to witness the grandest spectacle in sport - the FIFA World Cup. But among all its editions, there are a few that transcend time. Spain 1982 was one of them.

It was a tournament of transformation. The world was shifting - politically, culturally, emotionally - and football mirrored that change. For the first time, 24 nations stood shoulder to shoulder, expanding the canvas of competition and welcoming new voices to the global narrative. From the samba rhythms of Brazil to the cold discipline of West Germany, from the fire of Argentina to the quiet confidence of Italy, the tournament in Spain would come to embody everything football stands for: drama, joy, heartbreak, and glory.

Spain, newly reawakening from decades of authoritarian rule, offered itself as both host and symbol. It was a country in transition, much like the game itself. Its sunlit stadiums, from Bilbao to Seville, became arenas not only of sport but of identity, memory, and hope.

This is not merely a story of matches and goals. It is the story of a world coming together in 1982 - a world divided by ideologies but united by the love of the beautiful game. It is the story of stars who shone and dreams that shattered. It is the story of an orange mascot named Naranjito, of a bruising semifinal that shocked consciences, of a redemption arc carved by a man named Rossi, and of a scream that echoed through the ages - Tardelli's cry of triumph.

"Echoes of '82" invites you to step back into that sun-drenched summer, to feel the roar of the crowds, the sweat on the brows, and the heartbeat of a world captured by football. Turn the page, and return to a moment when the world stopped - and the game spoke.

Chapter 1: The World in Waiting

The year was 1982, and the world stood at a crossroads. The Cold War still divided East from West, with political tensions simmering between superpowers. Television sets beamed images of global conflict, economic hardship, and shifting alliances into households everywhere. Yet, amid the uncertainty and ideological stand-offs, there existed one common language that could still unify hearts across borders - football.

That summer, the eyes of millions turned toward a sun-drenched Spain, a country undergoing a profound transformation of its own. Less than a decade had passed since the death of General Francisco Franco, and Spain was still finding its voice in a new democratic age. The 1982 World Cup was more than a sporting event for the Iberian nation - it was a coming-out party, a declaration that Spain was ready to rejoin the world not just politically, but culturally and emotionally. With newly elected democratic leadership, modern infrastructure initiatives, and renewed ties to Western Europe, Spain had taken bold steps to reshape its global image. Hosting the World Cup was the crown jewel in this effort.

The preparation had been immense. Stadiums were renovated and expanded. Roads and rail networks were upgraded. Tourism campaigns promised sunny beaches, vibrant culture, and footballing passion. The mascot, Naranjito - a cheerful orange donning a Spanish kit - became a symbol of both youthful joy and national optimism. From Seville's sweltering afternoons to the cooler northern city of Gijón, the country buzzed with excitement and nervous pride.

For football fans around the world, anticipation grew. The tournament's expansion to 24 teams promised more matches, more goals, and more drama. It also meant new stories. For the first time, countries like Algeria, Cameroon, Honduras, and New Zealand would join the global stage, each carrying the hopes and pride of their people. Meanwhile, the old powers - Brazil, Argentina, Italy, England, West Germany - arrived with dreams of glory and a burden of expectation.

The defending champions, Argentina, were led by César Luis Menotti, the philosopher-coach who had won the tournament in 1978 on home soil. This time, however, all eyes were on a prodigious 21-year-old named Diego Armando Maradona. His debut on football's biggest stage was one of the most eagerly anticipated moments of the tournament. Little did anyone know that Spain 1982 would test his temperament more than his talent.

Brazil, with its flowing football and attacking flair, arrived as favorites. Their midfield - composed of the cerebral Sócrates, the dazzling Zico, and the powerful Falcão - promised to mesmerize. The press dubbed them "the team of the decade" even before a ball had been kicked. In contrast, Italy arrived under a cloud of skepticism. Their striker Paolo Rossi had just returned from a two-year suspension due to a match-fixing scandal. The Italian public was divided - some hopeful, others resentful. Few could have predicted the redemption story that was about to unfold.

Elsewhere, England returned to the World Cup for the first time since 1970, with hopes resting on the shoulders of Kevin Keegan and Trevor Francis. France, led by the elegant Michel Platini, hoped to blend artistry with steel. West Germany, ever efficient and composed, were quietly confident, even as they were burdened by high expectations at home.

In the weeks leading up to the tournament, the world press filled columns with speculation. Who would lift the trophy? Could the hosts make a deep run? Would Brazil's samba style triumph, or would European pragmatism prevail? In cafés, pubs, and living rooms across the globe, fans debated lineups, referees, and star players. Football fever was everywhere.

But amid the excitement, there was also tension. In the South Atlantic, the Falklands War raged between Argentina and the

United Kingdom. Though the conflict would not directly interfere with the matches, its shadow loomed large. The war, which began just months before the tournament, created an emotional divide, particularly in the matches involving those nations. Even within the sacred arena of sport, politics was never far behind.

As kickoff approached, the host cities braced for the influx of players, journalists, and fans. Barcelona, Madrid, Valencia, Bilbao, Seville - each offered a distinct regional flavor, giving the tournament a diverse texture unlike any before. The majestic Camp Nou, the historic Santiago Bernabéu, and the newly modernized Estadio Benito Villamarín stood ready to host moments that would be etched into the collective memory of the footballing world.

The opening match was scheduled for June 13, and the world waited. Across time zones and languages, people marked their calendars, stocked their fridges, and prepared for a month of spectacle. As the teams trained behind closed doors, as flags were hoisted and anthems rehearsed, one truth became clear: the stage was set, and history was about to unfold.

Spain 1982 would be more than a tournament. It would be a mirror to the world - its triumphs, its contradictions, its unity, and its divisions. And as the first whistle echoed across Camp Nou, it was not just a game that had begun, but a story that would be told for generations.

Chapter 2: Setting the Stage

The sun rose over the Iberian Peninsula on the morning of June 13, 1982, casting long golden rays across the mosaic of stadiums that would soon become arenas of hope and heartbreak. It was the dawn of the most ambitious World Cup in history. For the first time, the tournament featured 24 national teams, a decision made by FIFA not only to expand the reach of the game but to symbolize the growing universality of football. More than ever, the World Cup was a celebration of cultures, styles, and stories converging into a single global spectacle.

The decision to include more teams reshaped the format entirely. The tournament began with six groups of four, from which the top two teams would progress to a second group stage-an unusual and short-lived design that confused many fans and players alike. Instead of proceeding directly to knockouts, teams would again be placed into groups in the second round, with only the group winners advancing to the semifinals. It was complex, sometimes frustrating, but undeniably dramatic.

Each of the 24 teams arrived in Spain with unique aspirations and burdens. Some came as giants, others as hopeful underdogs, and a few as mere representatives of emerging football cultures. But all came with a dream.

Group 1 featured the host nation, Spain, along with Honduras, Yugoslavia, and Northern Ireland. The pressure on the hosts was immense. Their squad, led by veterans like Santillana and Quini, was expected to perform well, if not go all the way. But they faced stiff challenges, particularly from a spirited Northern Ireland side and a Yugoslavian team rich with technical prowess. Honduras, in their debut appearance, were unknown but determined to prove they belonged.

Group 2 placed Algeria, West Germany, Austria, and Chile in a group that would become infamous by the end. West Germany entered as favorites, but Algeria stunned the world with a 2-1 victory in their opening match. It was a result that would later be overshadowed by controversy-a topic that would shake the foundations of the tournament's sporting spirit.

Group 3 showcased Argentina, Belgium, El Salvador, and Hungary. Argentina were defending champions, but despite their pedigree, Belgium stunned them in the tournament opener. El Salvador's participation marked a proud moment for Central America, though their 10-1 loss to Hungary would remain one of the tournament's most lopsided results. That match also saw Laszlo Kiss record the first-ever World Cup hat-trick by a substitute.

Group 4 included England, France, Czechoslovakia, and Kuwait. England's return to the World Cup was long-awaited, and they made an immediate impression. France, led by Platini, had flashes of brilliance, but their inconsistencies would haunt them. Kuwait, making their debut, faced a tough learning curve but left a memorable mark thanks to a bizarre moment involving a royal family member and a referee.

Group 5 brought together Spain's linguistic cousins Brazil, alongside the Soviet Union, Scotland, and New Zealand. Brazil dazzled from the first kick, treating fans to flowing, expressive football that seemed more art than sport. Zico, Sócrates, Éder, and Falcão became the names on every commentator's lips. Scotland once again brought hope and heartbreak, and New Zealand, in their first-ever World Cup, fought valiantly despite heavy defeats.

Group 6 paired Italy, Poland, Peru, and Cameroon. Italy's form was dreadful in the group stage-three uninspired draws that left fans and pundits questioning their very presence in the tournament. Paolo Rossi, the controversial inclusion, looked out of place and off-form. Cameroon, on the other hand, earned respect with their discipline and heart, exiting the tournament unbeaten after three draws.

Each group offered its own storylines, heroes, and disappointments. From the exuberance of debutants to the tactical rigidity of the European giants, Spain 1982 was becoming a canvas on which contrasting footballing philosophies clashed. It was a World Cup of experimentation-not just tactically, but structurally and emotionally.

The matches were played in cities rich with culture and history. In Seville, fans sizzled under the Andalusian sun as they watched tempers flare and goals fly. In Bilbao, the Basque crowd lent an electric intensity to matches, often cheering with more passion than neutrality. In Madrid, the capital's grand Santiago Bernabéu stood as the centerpiece of the competition, promising to host its climactic final. Barcelona's Camp Nou hosted the opener and brought its own regal presence, befitting the grandeur of the tournament.

The officiating, too, became a topic of discussion. As the tournament unfolded, strange decisions, unpunished fouls, and controversial goals added to the drama. While some referees sought to preserve the flow of matches, others cracked down, often inconsistently. FIFA's protocols were under scrutiny, especially as the stakes rose and tempers frayed.

Behind the scenes, logistical coordination was a Herculean task. With 24 teams, thousands of support staff, and hundreds of journalists descending on the country, Spain's transport, accommodation, and security services were pushed to their limits. Yet the vibrancy of the tournament never waned. Fans filled plazas, beaches, and boulevards in a continuous festival that spilled far beyond the stadiums. Naranjito merchandise filled shop windows, and children mimicked their favorite players in cobblestone alleyways and sun-scorched courtyards.

As the group stages progressed, certain narratives began to emerge: Italy's unconvincing start; Brazil's breathtaking performances; Argentina's unpredictability; and the possibility of another deep run for West Germany. But for all the projections and predictions, nothing could prepare the world for what the second round would bring.

Because just as the group stage had introduced the characters and laid the setting, the next chapter - the second group stage - would deliver the drama. And it would all begin with a match that would haunt football history for decades.

Introduction: The Summer That Changed Everything

In the blistering heat of a Spanish summer, as guitars played in smoky taverns and the scent of oranges drifted through narrow streets, the world came together - not for war, not for politics, but for a game. The year was 1982, and the World Cup was more than just a tournament. It was a stage for drama, for artistry, for heartbreak, and for glory.

Spain, newly reborn from the shadows of dictatorship, opened its arms to the globe. Across Seville, Barcelona, Madrid, and Bilbao, stadiums pulsed with music, with chants, with color. For the first time, the World Cup would host 24 nations, an expanded format filled with hope and complexity. And into this vibrant canvas stepped legends - some at the height of their powers, others just beginning their myth.

Zico. Sócrates. Platini. Rummenigge. Rossi. Maradona.

Names that echoed across continents. Men who carried not just the weight of expectation but the dreams of millions.

This was a tournament of contradictions. Of samba and steel. Of genius and grit. Of beauty undone by ruthlessness. In these pages, you will not simply read about goals or tactics - you will feel the heat rising from the pitch, hear the roar of the crowds, and witness the moment when time seemed to stop.

This is the story of Spain '82 - the World Cup that gave us more than a champion. It gave us heroes and villains, art and agony, joy and injustice. It gave us echoes that still reverberate through football's soul.

This is not a chronicle.

It is a memory.

A living, breathing tribute to the tournament that changed

everything.

Chapter 9: After the Storm

As the celebrations echoed into the Madrid night and confetti clung to sweat-soaked jerseys, the world began to reflect on what had transpired in Spain. The 1982 World Cup had been more than a tournament - it had been a theater of emotion, a collision of eras, a mirror of humanity. And once the noise faded and the stadiums emptied, what remained were the stories: of resilience, redemption, controversy, and dreams both realized and shattered.

Italy returned home to a hero's welcome. Their streets flooded with jubilant fans, and their blue jerseys became symbols of national pride. For a country recently marred by political instability and scandal, the triumph offered unity, hope, and renewal. Paolo Rossi, once disgraced, was now adored. He had finished the tournament as top scorer with six goals - all in the final three matches. His transformation from exile to icon was the beating heart of Italy's story.

Coach Enzo Bearzot, dignified and unflinching, had vindicated his vision. He had trusted in character as much as talent, and the results had been emphatic. His refusal to bend to the media's pressure made him both controversial and courageous. In many ways, his Italy had not just won - they had overcome.

West Germany, though defeated, left with heads held high. Their run to the final was defined by drama, determination, and an unbreakable will. The semifinal against France would go down in history as one of the greatest - and most controversial - matches ever played. Yet even in the face of criticism, they had demonstrated the depth and steel that defined German football.

France, meanwhile, mourned a dream lost. The images of Battiston's unconscious body, Platini's tears, and Giresse's heartbreak lingered in the public conscience. But Les Bleus had also announced their arrival. Their style, their courage, and their character had earned global admiration. For Platini, this would be the first step in a legendary career.

Brazil's 1982 squad remained a paradox - arguably the best team not to win a World Cup. The world had danced to their rhythm, only to mourn their fall. Their elimination did not diminish their brilliance; rather, it immortalized it. In every street game and conversation that followed, people would speak of Zico's finesse, Sócrates' elegance, Falcão's drive. They had elevated football to poetry - and left the tournament with grace.

For others - Algeria, Cameroon, Northern Ireland - Spain 1982 had been a platform for respect and recognition. Algeria's defeat of West Germany and their unjust exit prompted FIFA to change its tournament scheduling forever, ensuring final group matches were played simultaneously. Cameroon left unbeaten, a sign of the African footballing revolution on the horizon. Northern Ireland's stunning victory over the hosts reminded the world that passion could topple giants.

Even the host nation, Spain, though disappointed in their team's performance, proved themselves as gracious and capable organizers. The tournament had unfolded smoothly, and their cultural warmth had colored the event with personality and joy. From Bilbao's fervent crowds to Seville's late-night serenades, Spain had shown the world its heart.

And for FIFA, the expansion to 24 teams had offered both promise and problems. It had brought new faces and fresh energy, but also logistical confusion and questionable structures. Still, it marked the beginning of a more global, more inclusive World Cup - a legacy that would shape the tournaments to come.

As the summer faded, so too did the immediate intensity of the World Cup. But its echoes endured. In every replayed goal, every argument in bars and cafés, every playground dream of becoming the next Rossi or Platini, Spain 1982 lived on.

It was not just a moment in football. It was a mosaic of life.

Chapter 10: Legacy of '82

The final whistle had long blown, but Spain 1982 refused to fade. It lingered - in memory, in myth, and in the marrow of football itself. Long after the goals had been scored and the champions crowned, the tournament lived on as one of the most defining and dramatic chapters in the history of the beautiful game.

Legacy is not always about statistics. It is about feeling. And the feeling left behind by the 1982 World Cup was one of awe, complexity, and transformation. It was a turning point. A passage between two footballing eras - from the rigid tactics of old to the creative explosion of the modern game.

For Italy, it was the moment their footballing soul was reborn. The 1982 squad became legends. Paolo Rossi's resurrection remains one of the sport's most powerful redemption stories. His name would forever be associated with clutch performance and poetic justice. Dino Zoff, lifting the trophy at 40, became a symbol of endurance and leadership. Marco Tardelli's scream after his goal in the final remains one of football's purest expressions of triumph.

But beyond Italy, the tournament left fingerprints on the global game. France's heartbreak in Seville would forge a generation hungry for redemption, culminating in their own triumph in 1998. Brazil, wounded yet adored, would return with vengeance in future tournaments. Germany - consistent, powerful, and relentless - reaffirmed their role as perennial contenders.

Spain 1982 also accelerated football's globalization. The debut of nations like Algeria, Cameroon, and New Zealand opened the door to a more inclusive tournament structure. It proved that football's magic was not confined to Europe or South America. The sport was growing. Fast.

Tactically, the tournament prompted introspection. Brazil's elimination despite playing the most exciting football reignited the debate between style and substance. Could beauty win? Or must victory always belong to pragmatism? These questions would haunt football for decades, influencing philosophies from club academies to national programs.

Culturally, the tournament captured imaginations through television like never before. Spain 1982 reached homes in ways earlier tournaments could not. The vivid colors, the drama, the mascots, the emotion - it felt close, alive. Naranjito, the cartoon orange, became iconic. Broadcasts brought fans into stadiums, and with them came a new era of football consumption. The World Cup was no longer just an event - it was a global phenomenon.

And then there were the moments. The unforgettable. The controversial. The sublime. Schumacher and Battiston. Rossi's hat-trick. Tardelli's scream. Brazil's flowing brilliance. Algeria's pride. Northern Ireland's shock. The tears of Platini. The defiance of Zoff. The agony and the ecstasy. These were not just highlights - they were history.

Looking back, Spain 1982 didn't just belong to one nation. It belonged to everyone who watched, who cheered, who suffered and celebrated. It was proof that football is not merely a game. It is drama, art, struggle, and joy. It is the world in miniature, played out over grass and chalk lines.

Decades later, when people speak of the greatest World Cups ever played, Spain 1982 is always in the conversation. Not because it was perfect - but because it was human. In all its unpredictability, its flaws, its beauty - it captured what football truly is.

An echo. A memory. A feeling.

Spain 1982 lives on.

- END -

Chapter 3: The Opening Curtain

June 13, 1982. The summer heat shimmered above the sprawling roof of Barcelona's Camp Nou. The scent of sun-warmed concrete mixed with the aroma of fresh-cut grass as over 95,000 fans packed the stadium, many of them waving red-and-yellow flags or wearing the colors of their homeland. It was a day that promised spectacle, emotion, and the birth of new legends. The 12th FIFA World Cup was about to begin.

The honor of opening the tournament fell to the host nation, Spain, who faced off against debutants Honduras. Optimism filled the Spanish air. This was meant to be a celebration - a confident stride into a new democratic era, a unifying event for a nation still grappling with regional divisions and political scars from its authoritarian past. But football, ever unpredictable, had its own script.

Spain struggled. Nervous and disjointed, their play lacked rhythm and confidence. The Honduran team, by contrast, played with a mix of freedom and discipline. In the 7th minute, they stunned the crowd when Héctor Zelaya scored after a slick move, silencing the stadium. Although Spain equalized through a penalty from López Ufarte, the 1-1 result felt more like a defeat than a draw for the hosts. The opening curtain had not revealed a dominant protagonist, but rather a story still full of uncertainty.

This surprising result set the tone for a tournament of unpredictable outcomes and shifting narratives.

Across the country, in the northern city of Gijón, the Algerian national team prepared for what many expected to be a routine victory for West Germany. But the Desert Foxes had no intention of playing the role of bystanders. With pace, tactical organization, and sheer belief, they defeated the two-time world champions 2-1 - one of the most shocking upsets in World Cup history. Goals from Rabah Madjer and Lakhdar Belloumi sent shockwaves through the footballing world.

Elsewhere, Brazil made its debut against the Soviet Union in Seville. It was a closely fought match, but Brazil's class emerged in the end with a 2-1 win, thanks to goals from Sócrates and Éder. The latter's thunderous strike from outside the box - hit with the outside of his left foot - was a goal that embodied the Brazilian soul: audacious, elegant, and unforgettable.

On June 15, Argentina, the reigning champions, entered the tournament with the eyes of the world upon them. In the spotlight: a 21-year-old prodigy named Diego Maradona. Facing Belgium in the tournament's opening night match in Barcelona, Argentina were expected to assert their authority. But Belgium executed a masterclass in containment. Maradona was harried and hacked, and despite flashes of brilliance, Argentina were subdued. Erwin Vandenbergh scored the match's only goal, and Argentina's title defense was off to a rocky start.

England, meanwhile, announced their return to World Cup football after a 12-year absence with the fastest goal of the tournament. In just 27 seconds, Bryan Robson volleyed home against France in Bilbao. The English went on to win 3-1, with Robson adding another and Paul Mariner sealing the result. It was a statement performance and a warning to the rest of the world.

But not all storylines were joyous. El Salvador endured a humiliating 10-1 defeat to Hungary, the most lopsided loss in World Cup history at the time. The Hungarian team, spearheaded by Tibor Nyilasi and Laszlo Kiss, showed no mercy. Kiss's second-half hat-trick - achieved in under ten minutes - was the first ever by a substitute at a World Cup. For El Salvador, it was a painful moment on the world stage, but one that still drew admiration for their courage to compete.

Drama was not limited to the pitch. In the match between France and Kuwait, chaos ensued when a whistle from the stands caused several French players to halt during an attacking move. France scored a goal, but the Kuwaitis protested vehemently. In an unprecedented moment, Prince Fahad Al-Ahmad, brother of the Emir and president of the Kuwaiti FA, came down from the stands, onto the pitch, and demanded the goal be disallowed. Shockingly, the referee - under pressure - overturned the decision. France still won 4-1, but the incident sparked international debate about interference and integrity in sport.

Back in Group 1, Spain's next match against Yugoslavia offered a chance for redemption. They managed a narrow 2-1 win, easing national anxiety. But their final group match against Northern Ireland would turn into one of the great upsets of the tournament. In Valencia, Gerry Armstrong's goal secured a stunning 1-0 win, topping the group and sending shockwaves through Europe. Northern Ireland's amateurs had defeated the proud hosts - a result that would live long in football folklore.

Cameroon, another debutant, played with heart and resilience in Group 6. Though they didn't win a single match, they held Poland, Peru, and even Italy to draws - and exited the tournament unbeaten. Their solid defending, represented by the leadership of goalkeeper Thomas N'Kono, earned them global respect and paved the way for future African teams.

The group stage's closing acts brought both celebration and controversy. West Germany and Austria faced each other in a match that would come to be known as the "Disgrace of Gijón." A 1-0 win for West Germany would ensure both teams advanced - and after an early goal, neither side attempted to score again. The spectacle of players simply passing the ball around drew jeers and outrage from fans and commentators. Algeria, who had fought valiantly and won two of their three games, were eliminated as a result. The fallout from that day would lead FIFA to change the scheduling format in future tournaments to ensure final group matches were played simultaneously.

By the end of the group stage, the 24 teams had become 12. The surprises, the heartbreaks, the new heroes - all had laid the groundwork for what was to come. The second round would bring fire and fury, tactical brilliance, and historic moments.

As the lights dimmed on the group stage and rose on the next act, one truth stood tall: the 1982 World Cup had already exceeded expectations. But its most unforgettable chapters were yet to be written.

Chapter 4: Maradona's Debut

It was perhaps the most anticipated debut in World Cup history. A boy from Villa Fiorito, with unruly curls and a left foot that whispered magic, was about to step onto football's greatest stage. Diego Armando Maradona, only 21 years old, carried with him the hopes of a nation and the weight of expectation that bordered on myth. Argentina's campaign in Spain 1982 was supposed to mark the ascent of a prodigy to the throne of global football. What followed was far more complex - a journey of brilliance and frustration, promise and punishment.

Argentina entered the tournament as defending champions, having triumphed on home soil in 1978. But this was a different side, facing a different challenge. They were no longer playing with the comfort of the crowd behind them, and the South American giants now had a reputation to uphold. Maradona was the jewel in César Luis Menotti's crown, but the team also featured veteran players like Daniel Passarella, Osvaldo Ardiles, and Leopoldo Luque - men who had seen glory before and now hoped to guide their younger teammates through the cauldron.

The opening match against Belgium was set under the bright lights of Camp Nou, and anticipation surged through the veins of supporters and neutrals alike. Maradona dazzled in the warm-ups, his touch electric, his balance supernatural. But the Belgians had studied him. They formed a tight ring around the number 10, rarely allowing him space to breathe, let alone create. Despite Argentina's possession and pressing, it was Belgium who struck. Erwin Vandenbergh scored the only goal of the game, and just like that, the holders were humbled.

Maradona showed glimpses of his genius - quick turns, feints, and mesmerizing dribbles - but also signs of immaturity. Frustrated by the tight marking and hard challenges, his temper simmered close to the surface. The legend was stirring, but it had not yet been born.

Their second match, against Hungary, offered a better canvas for Diego to paint on. With more space and a less aggressive opponent, Maradona thrived. He scored twice in a 4-1 win that restored Argentine morale. His first goal was a moment of beauty - a run that split defenders, followed by a clinical finish with his magical left foot. The second, a close-range finish, showcased his anticipation and killer instinct.

Then came El Salvador, and a more restrained but professional performance from the Albiceleste. They won 2-0 and qualified for the second round. Argentina seemed to be finding their rhythm. But the next stage would bring them face-to-face with two formidable adversaries: Italy and Brazil.

Against Italy, Maradona found himself the target of Enzo Bearzot's suffocating tactics. Claudio Gentile, Italy's notorious hard man, followed Diego relentlessly, often bending the limits of legality. Gentile's infamous quote after the match - "Football is not for ballerinas" - said it all. Maradona was kicked, pulled, and blocked at every turn. Italy won 2-1, and Diego, visibly enraged, finished the match in silence.

Then came Brazil. A dream matchup. The poets versus the fire. The old rivals. Brazil played with flowing elegance, and Argentina tried to respond with grit and flashes of genius. But the match quickly turned. Brazil dominated possession, and Maradona, desperate to make an impact, became more reckless. After a harsh tackle on Batista, Diego saw red - a straight dismissal. He left the field not with the glory many expected, but with his head bowed and his dreams postponed.

Argentina's title defense was over. Maradona's World Cup debut had ended in disillusionment. For all his talent, Spain 1982 revealed that even the brightest stars must grow through shadows. It would take four more years - and a different tournament - for Maradona to fulfill his destiny.

But even in disappointment, there was no doubt: the world had seen something different. Something rare. Maradona was not just another player. He was a force - raw, volatile, luminous. Spain was his first taste of the World Cup's fire. The world would never be the same again.

Chapter 5: The Samba Show

There is a certain rhythm to Brazilian football - a tempo that pulses beneath the surface, a dance between freedom and precision. In Spain 1982, Brazil's national team arrived not just to win, but to enchant. This was not merely a squad. It was an orchestra. And at its heart was a generation of artists in boots: Sócrates, Zico, Falcão, Éder, Toninho Cerezo. They came to play football the way composers write music - with elegance, spontaneity, and the power to move.

Their first match, a 2-1 win over the Soviet Union, had already shown glimpses of their brilliance. But it was only the beginning. In their next group games, Brazil unleashed a brand of football that captured the imagination of millions. Against Scotland, they dazzled. A 4-1 victory saw goals from Zico, Oscar, Éder, and Falcão. The movement, the passing, the flair - it was football as performance art.

New Zealand were next, and the result was inevitable. A 4-0 demolition. The crowd in Seville was mesmerized. Zico scored twice, while Falcão and Éder added to the spectacle. The goals were not just scored - they were crafted. Every pass, every flick, every feint seemed infused with joy. Commentators ran out of superlatives. The world had fallen in love.

But beauty alone does not win World Cups.

Brazil advanced to the second round, where they were placed in a group with old rivals Argentina and a struggling Italian side. On paper, it looked like a formality. In reality, it became one of the most memorable chapters in football history.

The clash against Argentina was highly anticipated - a battle between South American giants. Brazil dominated. From the outset, their superiority was clear. Zico opened the scoring with a brilliant finish, then Serginho doubled the lead. The midfield trio of Sócrates, Falcão, and Cerezo controlled every inch of the pitch.

Maradona, frustrated and isolated, was eventually sent off. Brazil won 3-1 and sent a message to the world: they were ready to reclaim their crown.

Then came Italy. July 5, 1982. Estadio Sarrià in Barcelona.

Italy had limped through the group stage with three draws. They had barely qualified. Their striker, Paolo Rossi, was being called a ghost by the Italian press. No one - not even many Italians - expected them to survive Brazil's samba storm.

But this was football.

The match began with fireworks. Rossi scored in the 5th minute, shocking the crowd. Brazil responded through Sócrates - a glorious, low finish after a clever pass from Zico. But Italy struck again. A poor clearance gifted Rossi a second goal. 2-1. Brazil pressed, passed, flowed. Éder hit the bar. Falcão equalized with a thunderous left-footed drive. 2-2. The game was a masterpiece.

Then came the dagger.

In the 74th minute, Rossi completed his hat-trick. A scrambled corner, a loose ball, and the man who had been forgotten became the man who would not be.

Brazil attacked with desperation and flair. But it was not enough. Italy won 3-2. Brazil - the most beautiful team of the tournament - were gone.

Tears fell across Brazil. Not just from players, but from fans around the world who had believed in their dream. For many, that 1982 team remains the greatest never to win the World Cup. They changed what people thought football could be.

Zico would later say, "We lost the World Cup, but we won the hearts of the world." He was right. The samba show had ended, but its echoes would live on.

Chapter 6: Italy Awakens

If football teaches us anything, it is that form is fleeting, but resolve is eternal. No team embodied this truth in 1982 more than Italy. Arriving in Spain under a cloud of controversy, lacking spark and public confidence, the Azzurri were seen by many as a team already defeated before the first whistle. But deep within this wounded squad lay the heart of a champion - one that would not only awaken, but roar.

Italy's preparation had been far from ideal. The team's talismanic striker, Paolo Rossi, had only just returned from a two-year suspension following the Totonero match-fixing scandal. Critics questioned his fitness, his sharpness, even his right to be there. The Italian media were relentless in their scrutiny. Enzo Bearzot, the stoic and principled coach, faced immense pressure and even refused to speak to the press during the group stage. He trusted his players and his vision - a trust that, at first, seemed misplaced.

In Group 1, Italy stumbled through three uninspiring draws. A 0-0 with Poland, a scrappy 1-1 against Peru, and another 1-1 with Cameroon. They advanced to the next round not by brilliance, but by goal difference. The critics sharpened their knives. The Italian public turned away. It appeared that the Azzurri's tournament would end in quiet embarrassment.

Then, something changed.

In the second round, Italy found themselves in Group C alongside two giants - Argentina and Brazil. The so-called "Group of Death." Most predicted a swift and painful exit. But Bearzot's men, hardened by adversity, had other ideas. And it began with Maradona's Argentina.

On July 2 in Barcelona, Italy took the field against the reigning champions. It was a different team - hungrier, more aggressive, united. Marco Tardelli was tireless in midfield. Claudio Gentile shadowed Maradona with ruthless discipline. And Rossi - the forgotten man - came to life. Though he didn't score, his movement unsettled the Argentine defense. Goals from Tardelli and Cabrini secured a 2-1 win. Italy had arrived.

But the real test - and one of the most famous matches in World Cup history - came three days later.

July 5, 1982. Italy vs Brazil. Estadio Sarrià.

Brazil were the favorites. Their football was flowing, poetic, breathtaking. Italy's play was pragmatic, efficient, almost mechanical. But as the game unfolded, it became clear: this was no mismatch. This was a clash of philosophies, and Italy's was about to prevail.

Paolo Rossi scored first - a poacher's finish. Sócrates equalized with flair. Then Rossi again, capitalizing on a defensive error. Falcão drew Brazil level once more with a thunderous strike. 2-2. The world held its breath. And then, in the 74th minute, Rossi completed his hat-trick. The stadium erupted. Italy, against all odds, had conquered the team considered the best in the world.

It was not just a win. It was a transformation. From then on, Italy were unstoppable.

In the semifinals, they faced Poland, a disciplined and dangerous side. Rossi struck twice, and Italy advanced with composure and confidence. He was now the tournament's top scorer, the hero Italy didn't know it still had.

Behind him, Dino Zoff - at 40 years old - led from the back with unmatched calm. Gaetano Scirea orchestrated the defense with elegance, and Gentile and Cabrini fought for every inch. Tardelli, Antognoni, and Conti ran the midfield with discipline and heart. Bearzot's system was peaking at the perfect moment.

Italy had not just awakened. They had evolved.

From disgraced and doubted to determined and defiant, the Azzurri were now just one step away from glory. And at their center was a man who had come to symbolize their entire journey: Paolo Rossi - resurrected, relentless, and ready.

Chapter 7: A Tale of Tragedy and Triumph

July 8, 1982. Ramón Sánchez Pizjuán Stadium, Seville. The evening heat was heavy, the atmosphere electric. Two European powerhouses - France and West Germany - prepared to battle for a place in the World Cup final. What followed would be one of the most extraordinary matches in the history of the sport: a story of beauty and brutality, of dreams raised and crushed, of glory denied and infamy earned.

France had emerged as one of the tournament's most stylish teams, their midfield trio of Michel Platini, Alain Giresse, and Jean Tigana playing with grace and flair. They were the romantic choice - poetic, technical, and unpredictable. West Germany, in contrast, embodied efficiency and grit. Led by Karl-Heinz Rummenigge and captained by the indomitable Paul Breitner, they were disciplined and determined.

The match began with intensity. Pierre Littbarski opened the scoring for West Germany, but France responded with a penalty from Platini, making it 1-1. The game flowed back and forth, tactical yet passionate, with moments of brilliance on both sides.

But then came a moment that cast a long shadow over the match - and over football history.

In the second half, French substitute Patrick Battiston latched onto a through-ball from Platini and sprinted toward goal. As he flicked the ball past Harald Schumacher, the German goalkeeper charged out with terrifying force. He leapt into Battiston with his hip and forearm, knocking the Frenchman unconscious before he could even hit the ground.

Battiston lay motionless. Teeth knocked out. Neck injured. Unconscious. The stadium fell silent.

Incredibly, no foul was given. No card. No penalty. Nothing.

It was a moment of raw violence and shocking inaction.

Schumacher's lack of concern and the referee's decision not to penalize the foul infuriated fans and commentators alike. To this day, it remains one of the most controversial moments in World Cup history.

The match continued, but it was now haunted by what had transpired.

In extra time, France seemed to rise above the pain. They scored twice - a magnificent team goal finished by Marius Trésor, followed by a delicate strike from Alain Giresse. 3-1. It appeared they were on their way to the final.

But the Germans refused to surrender.

Karl-Heinz Rummenigge, introduced off the bench, scored to make it 3-2. Then, in the 108th minute, Klaus Fischer equalized with an acrobatic overhead kick. 3-3. The momentum had shifted.

For the first time in World Cup history, a semifinal would be decided by penalties.

The shootout was tense, dramatic, and agonizing. Uli Stielike missed for West Germany, breaking down in tears, but Schumacher redeemed himself - saving from Didier Six and then from Maxime Bossis. Horst Hrubesch converted the final kick. West Germany had won.

France were heartbroken. They had led, they had dazzled, and they had suffered. But they would not reach the final.

Across Spain, meanwhile, Italy prepared for their own semifinal against Poland. It was a calmer affair, though no less significant. Paolo Rossi struck twice - continuing his astonishing form - and Italy won 2-0, advancing to their first World Cup final since 1970.

One semifinal had delivered high drama and tragedy. The other, a confident step toward redemption.

As the dust settled, the stage was set: Italy vs West Germany in

Madrid. Two old rivals. Two proud footballing nations. But before that final whistle could blow, the world would pause to absorb the shock and emotion of what had just unfolded in Seville.

Spain 1982 was no longer just a tournament. It was becoming legend.

Chapter 8: The Grand Finale

July 11, 1982. Santiago Bernabéu Stadium, Madrid. The Spanish sun beat down upon a world holding its breath. For a month, 24 teams had fought across cities and stadiums, dreams made and broken beneath the Iberian skies. Now, only two remained: Italy and West Germany. Titans of European football. Familiar foes. It was a final worthy of the journey.

The Santiago Bernabéu buzzed with anticipation. Over 90,000 fans filled the stands, flags waving, chants echoing, and nerves taut. The atmosphere was electric. In the presence of kings, presidents, and football royalty, the two finalists walked onto the pitch. Italy in blue, calm and focused. West Germany in white, determined and proud. At stake: a third World Cup title for either side - and eternal glory.

The match began tentatively. Nerves showed on both sides. In the 23rd minute, Italy were awarded a penalty after Bruno Conti was brought down inside the box. The responsibility fell to Antonio Cabrini. He stepped up, the tension palpable - and missed. The ball sailed wide. A collective gasp filled the stadium. Italy's chance for an early advantage had vanished.

But they did not crumble. If anything, it galvanized them.

Dino Zoff, Italy's veteran goalkeeper and captain at age 40, organized the defense with masterful authority. Gaetano Scirea was flawless in the backline. Gentile, Cabrini, and Collovati worked tirelessly to deny Rummenigge and Littbarski any space.

In midfield, Marco Tardelli, Bruno Conti, and Gabriele Oriali began to take control. The ball moved with purpose now. Confidence grew. Then, in the 57th minute, the moment arrived.

Claudio Gentile burst down the right, swinging a cross into the box. Marco Tardelli slid the ball to the center. Paolo Rossi, the man of the hour, rose above the German defenders and headed the ball past Schumacher. 1-0. His sixth goal of the tournament. The redemption arc was complete. From scandal to stardom, Rossi had etched his name into World Cup folklore.

Italy were flying. Just twelve minutes later, the second goal arrived, and it brought with it one of the most iconic celebrations in football history.

Tardelli received the ball at the edge of the box. One touch to settle, another to strike - left foot, low and precise, past Schumacher. Goal. 2-0.

And then came the scream.

Tardelli sprinted away, fists clenched, face contorted in raw, unfiltered emotion. Tears streamed down his cheeks as he screamed into the sky. It was not joy. It was catharsis. Decades of effort, sacrifice, pressure, and doubt exploded in that moment. The image would become immortal.

West Germany, stunned, tried to respond. But Italy were now unstoppable. In the 81st minute, Alessandro Altobelli added a third. A clean finish after a sweeping move - the final nail in the German coffin.

Paul Breitner scored a late consolation goal for West Germany, making it 3-1. But the match was done. Italy had conquered.

When the final whistle blew, the Bernabéu erupted. President Sandro Pertini stood in the stands, fists raised, beaming with pride. Bearzot and his players embraced in disbelief and euphoria. Paolo Rossi wept. Dino Zoff lifted the World Cup trophy high - the oldest player ever to do so.

Italy were champions of the world for the third time, joining Brazil as the only nation with such a distinction. But this was more than a victory. It was a resurrection.

Spain 1982 had delivered a final of passion and perfection. A team that had been doubted, scorned, and written off had risen.

And in doing so, they had reminded the world of what football can mean - not just as a sport, but as a story.

[Chapter 9 follows]

Chapter 9: After the Storm

As the celebrations echoed into the Madrid night and confetti clung to sweat-soaked jerseys, the world began to reflect on what had transpired in Spain. The 1982 World Cup had been more than a tournament - it had been a theater of emotion, a collision of eras, a mirror of humanity. And once the noise faded and the stadiums emptied, what remained were the stories: of resilience, redemption, controversy, and dreams both realized and shattered.

Italy returned home to a hero's welcome. Their streets flooded with jubilant fans, and their blue jerseys became symbols of national pride. For a country recently marred by political instability and scandal, the triumph offered unity, hope, and renewal. Paolo Rossi, once disgraced, was now adored. He had finished the tournament as top scorer with six goals - all in the final three matches. His transformation from exile to icon was the beating heart of Italy's story.

Coach Enzo Bearzot, dignified and unflinching, had vindicated his vision. He had trusted in character as much as talent, and the results had been emphatic. His refusal to bend to the media's pressure made him both controversial and courageous. In many ways, his Italy had not just won - they had overcome.

West Germany, though defeated, left with heads held high. Their run to the final was defined by drama, determination, and an unbreakable will. The semifinal against France would go down in history as one of the greatest - and most controversial - matches ever played. Yet even in the face of criticism, they had demonstrated the depth and steel that defined German football.

France, meanwhile, mourned a dream lost. The images of Battiston's unconscious body, Platini's tears, and Giresse's heartbreak lingered in the public conscience. But Les Bleus had also announced their arrival. Their style, their courage, and their character had earned global admiration. For Platini, this would be the first step in a legendary career.

Brazil's 1982 squad remained a paradox - arguably the best team not to win a World Cup. The world had danced to their rhythm, only to mourn their fall. Their elimination did not diminish their brilliance; rather, it immortalized it. In every street game and conversation that followed, people would speak of Zico's finesse, Sócrates' elegance, Falcão's drive. They had elevated football to poetry - and left the tournament with grace.

For others - Algeria, Cameroon, Northern Ireland - Spain 1982 had been a platform for respect and recognition. Algeria's defeat of West Germany and their unjust exit prompted FIFA to change its tournament scheduling forever, ensuring final group matches were played simultaneously. Cameroon left unbeaten, a sign of the African footballing revolution on the horizon. Northern Ireland's stunning victory over the hosts reminded the world that passion could topple giants.

Even the host nation, Spain, though disappointed in their team's performance, proved themselves as gracious and capable organizers. The tournament had unfolded smoothly, and their cultural warmth had colored the event with personality and joy. From Bilbao's fervent crowds to Seville's late-night serenades, Spain had shown the world its heart.

And for FIFA, the expansion to 24 teams had offered both promise and problems. It had brought new faces and fresh energy, but also logistical confusion and questionable structures. Still, it marked the beginning of a more global, more inclusive World Cup - a legacy that would shape the tournaments to come.

As the summer faded, so too did the immediate intensity of the World Cup. But its echoes endured. In every replayed goal, every argument in bars and cafés, every playground dream of becoming the next Rossi or Platini, Spain 1982 lived on.

It was not just a moment in football. It was a mosaic of life.

Chapter 10: Legacy of '82

The final whistle had long blown, but Spain 1982 refused to fade. It lingered - in memory, in myth, and in the marrow of football itself. Long after the goals had been scored and the champions crowned, the tournament lived on as one of the most defining and dramatic chapters in the history of the beautiful game.

Legacy is not always about statistics. It is about feeling. And the feeling left behind by the 1982 World Cup was one of awe, complexity, and transformation. It was a turning point. A passage between two footballing eras - from the rigid tactics of old to the creative explosion of the modern game.

For Italy, it was the moment their footballing soul was reborn. The 1982 squad became legends. Paolo Rossi's resurrection remains one of the sport's most powerful redemption stories. His name would forever be associated with clutch performance and poetic justice. Dino Zoff, lifting the trophy at 40, became a symbol of endurance and leadership. Marco Tardelli's scream after his goal in the final remains one of football's purest expressions of triumph.

But beyond Italy, the tournament left fingerprints on the global game. France's heartbreak in Seville would forge a generation hungry for redemption, culminating in their own triumph in 1998. Brazil, wounded yet adored, would return with vengeance in future tournaments. Germany - consistent, powerful, and relentless - reaffirmed their role as perennial contenders.

Spain 1982 also accelerated football's globalization. The debut of nations like Algeria, Cameroon, and New Zealand opened the door to a more inclusive tournament structure. It proved that football's magic was not confined to Europe or South America. The sport was growing. Fast.

Tactically, the tournament prompted introspection. Brazil's elimination despite playing the most exciting football reignited the debate between style and substance. Could beauty win? Or must victory always belong to pragmatism? These questions would haunt football for decades, influencing philosophies from club academies to national programs.

Culturally, the tournament captured imaginations through television like never before. Spain 1982 reached homes in ways earlier tournaments could not. The vivid colors, the drama, the mascots, the emotion - it felt close, alive. Naranjito, the cartoon orange, became iconic. Broadcasts brought fans into stadiums, and with them came a new era of football consumption. The World Cup was no longer just an event - it was a global phenomenon.

And then there were the moments. The unforgettable. The controversial. The sublime. Schumacher and Battiston. Rossi's hat-trick. Tardelli's scream. Brazil's flowing brilliance. Algeria's pride. Northern Ireland's shock. The tears of Platini. The defiance of Zoff. The agony and the ecstasy. These were not just highlights - they were history.

Looking back, Spain 1982 didn't just belong to one nation. It belonged to everyone who watched, who cheered, who suffered and celebrated. It was proof that football is not merely a game. It is drama, art, struggle, and joy. It is the world in miniature, played out over grass and chalk lines.

Decades later, when people speak of the greatest World Cups ever played, Spain 1982 is always in the conversation. Not because it was perfect - but because it was human. In all its unpredictability, its flaws, its beauty - it captured what football truly is.

An echo. A memory. A feeling.

Spain 1982 lives on.

- END -

Printed in Dunstable, United Kingdom